Math in My World

Math on the Playground

By William Amato

Children's Press®
A Division of Scholastic Inc.
New York / Toronto / London / Auckland / Sydney
Mexico City / New Delhi / Hong Kong
Danbury, Connecticut

Photo Credits: Cover and all photos by Maura Boruchow
Contributing Editor: Jennifer Silate
Book Design: Laura Stein

Library of Congress Cataloging-in-Publication Data

Amato, William.
Math on the playground / by William Amato.
p. cm. -- (Math in my world)
Includes bibliographical references and index.
Summary: Shows fun ways to practice addition and subtraction on a visit to the playground.
ISBN 0-516-23938-4 (lib. bdg.) -- ISBN 0-516-23594-X (pbk.)
1. Mathematics--Juvenile literature. [1. Mathematics.] I. Title.

QA40.5 .A54 2002
513--dc21

2001032342

Printed in the United States of America.
1 2 3 4 5 6 7 8 9 10 R 11 10 09 08 07 06 05 04 03 02

Contents

Today, we are going to the **playground**.

We are riding our bikes.

Each bike has two wheels.

How many wheels are there?

We count the wheels on each bike.

There are eight wheels in all!

The **swing set** has four swings.

We sit on three of the swings.

How many more kids can swing with us?

One more kid can swing with us.

Now all four swings are filled!

The playground also has **monkey bars**.

There are fourteen bars.

Kim has gone eight bars.

How many more bars are left?

There are six bars left!

Kim has gone the rest of the way.

We use math on the playground.

Math is fun!

New Words

monkey bars (**mung**-kee **bars**) metal bars that are made for climbing and swinging

playground (**play**-grownd) a place where kids play on swing sets, slides, and monkey bars

swing set (**swihng seht**) a row of seats that are hooked onto chains that swing from a bar

To Find Out More

Books

Pigs on the Ball: Fun with Math and Sports
by Amy Axelrod
Simon & Schuster Children's Press

Just Add Fun!
by Joanne Rocklin
Scholastic, Inc.

Web Site

FunBrain
http://www.funbrain.com
Play math baseball, math car racing, and many other fun games on this Web site.

Index

About the Author

William Amato is a teacher and writer living in New York City.

Reading Consultants

Kris Flynn, Coordinator, Small School District Literacy, The San Diego County Office of Education

Shelly Forys, Certified Reading Recovery Specialist, W.J. Zahnow Elementary School, Waterloo, IL

Sue McAdams, Former President of the North Texas Reading Council of the IRA, and Early Literacy Consultant, Dallas, TX